# PODCAST GROWTH SECRETS

DIBAKAR BALA

Made with ♥ on the Notion Press Platform
www.notionpress.com

# Contents

# Contents

# A Secret Offer

Hey there,

Welcome to Podnity Family.

When we started Podcasting, there was nobody to guide us.

All we received was Criticism from Start to End.

We Tried, We Cried. But in the end, we Survived.

But it took us a 3 Years from 2018 to 2021.

We had the time to fail because the competition was non-existent.

Not Anymore.

The best time to become a Successful Podcaster was yesterday.

The next best is today.

And I don't want you to do it all by yourself.

*Send me a **Video of You with the Book** at hello@podnity.com and I'll send you back a **Secret Offer** in Return.*

Until we meet again, Happy Podcasting :)

# ONE

# Why Podcasting Is Blowing Up in India?

Podcasting, the digital audio medium that has been around for more than a decade, has started to gain popularity in India over the last few years. The growing number of Indian podcasters and the increasing number of listeners are proof that podcasting is blowing up in India. Here are some reasons why:

## *Rise of Mobile Internet Usage*

India has witnessed a significant rise in mobile internet usage in recent years, with affordable data plans and the availability of low-cost smartphones. According to a report by the Telecom Regulatory Authority of India (TRAI), India had over 750 million internet users as of 2020, and a majority of them access the internet on their mobile phones. With easy access to the internet, more and more Indians are discovering the world of podcasts.

### *Demand for Local Language Content*

India is a country with diverse languages and cultures, and podcasting has emerged as a platform to provide local language content to listeners. Many Indian podcasters are creating content in regional languages like Hindi, Marathi, Bengali, Tamil, and Telugu, among others. This has made podcasting more relatable and accessible to the Indian audience.

### *Growth of the Audio Entertainment Industry*

The audio entertainment industry in India is growing rapidly, with more people preferring audio content over traditional media like television and radio. This trend has created a demand for more audio content, and podcasting has filled that gap by providing a wide range of content in various genres like news, comedy, sports, and education, among others.

### *Increase in Commute Time*

India is a country with a large population, and traffic congestion is a significant problem in many cities. This has led to an increase in commute time, with people spending hours on the road. Podcasting has become a popular medium of entertainment and education for people during their commutes, making their travel time more productive and engaging.

### *Low Production Costs*

Podcasting is a relatively low-cost medium of content creation. With basic recording equipment and a quiet room, anyone can create a podcast. This has made podcasting accessible to everyone, including individuals and small businesses with limited budgets.

### *Growing Podcasting Ecosystem*

The Indian podcasting ecosystem is growing rapidly, with new podcasters, platforms, and advertisers entering the market. The government's initiatives to promote digital media and the growing interest of investors in the podcasting industry have given a boost to the podcasting ecosystem in India.

Podcasting is blowing up in India due to a combination of factors like the rise of mobile internet usage, demand for local language content, growth of the audio entertainment industry, increase in commute time, low production costs, and the growing podcasting ecosystem. With more and more people discovering the world of podcasts, the future of podcasting in India looks bright.

# TWO

# WHO SHOULD PODCAST?

If you are considering starting a podcast, you may be wondering if it's the right medium for you. The good news is that podcasting is a versatile platform that can be utilized by a wide range of people and businesses. In this chapter, we will discuss who should podcast and why.

## *Entrepreneurs and Business Owners*

Podcasting is an excellent way for entrepreneurs and business owners to showcase their expertise and connect with potential customers. Through podcasting, you can establish yourself as an authority in your field and build trust with your audience. Additionally, podcasting can help you reach a wider audience and generate leads for your business.

## *Creative Professionals*

Podcasting is an ideal medium for creative professionals, such as writers, filmmakers, and musicians, to showcase their work and connect with their audience. With podcasting, you can tell the story behind your creative process and share exclusive insights with your listeners.

### *Educators and Trainers*

Podcasting is an excellent tool for educators and trainers to reach a wider audience and share their knowledge. Through podcasting, you can create informative and engaging content that your students or trainees can listen to at their own pace.

### *Nonprofit Organizations*

Podcasting can be a powerful tool for nonprofit organizations to share their mission and raise awareness about their cause. By creating a podcast, you can engage with your supporters and share stories of the impact your organization is making.

### *Anyone with a Passion or Interest*

Finally, anyone with a passion or interest can start a podcast. Whether it's a hobby, a cause, or simply something you enjoy talking about, podcasting can be a great way to connect with like-minded people and share your ideas with the world.

In conclusion, podcasting is a medium that can be used by anyone who wants to connect with their audience, share their expertise or creativity, and build a community around their passion. Whether you are an entrepreneur, a creative professional, an educator, a nonprofit organization, or simply someone with a story to tell, podcasting is a platform that can help you reach your goals.

# THREE

# WHY SHOULD YOU PODCAST?

Podcasting has gained immense popularity in recent years, and for good reason. If you are considering starting a podcast, here are some reasons why it might be a great decision for you:

***Build Your Brand***

- Podcasting is an excellent way to build your personal or business brand. By sharing your thoughts, ideas, and expertise on a regular basis, you can establish yourself as an authority in your niche.
- Podcasting allows you to reach a wider audience and build a loyal following of listeners who value your content.
- By consistently producing valuable and engaging content, you can strengthen your relationship with your audience and position yourself as a thought leader in your industry.

### *Connect with Your Audience*

- Podcasting provides a unique opportunity to connect with your audience on a personal level. Listeners tend to feel a deeper connection with podcast hosts than they do with other types of content creators.
- With podcasting, you can create an intimate and conversational environment that encourages listeners to engage with you and each other.
- You can use your podcast to foster a community of like-minded individuals who share your interests and values.

### *Monetize Your Passion*

- Podcasting can be a lucrative source of income if done correctly. By building a loyal following of listeners, you can attract sponsorships, sell products or services, and even launch your own courses or coaching programs.
- Podcasting provides a platform for you to showcase your expertise and build trust with your audience, making it easier to sell your products or services.
- Unlike other forms of content creation, podcasting allows you to monetize your passion without relying solely on ad revenue.

### *Express Yourself*

- Podcasting allows you to express yourself in a way that is unique and authentic to you. You have the freedom to explore your interests and share your thoughts and ideas with your listeners.
- You can use your podcast to showcase your personality and creativity, and to experiment with different formats and topics.
- Podcasting provides a platform for you to share your stories and experiences with the world, and to make a positive impact on others.

### *Join a Growing Community*

- Podcasting is a rapidly growing medium, and by starting your own podcast, you can join a thriving community of podcasters.
- Podcasting provides opportunities to network with other content creators, learn from their experiences, and collaborate on projects.
- By joining the podcasting community, you can tap into a wealth of resources, tools, and knowledge that can help you grow and succeed as a podcaster.

In conclusion, podcasting offers a unique opportunity to build your brand, connect with your audience, monetize your passion, express yourself, and join a growing community of content creators. If any of these reasons resonate with you, then podcasting might be a great choice for you.

# FOUR

# Staying Consistent in Podcasting: Half the Battle

Podcasting has become a popular medium for creators to share their ideas, opinions, and stories with the world. However, the harsh reality is that most podcasts fail to stay consistent and don't make it past a few episodes. In fact, research shows that 90% of podcasts worldwide don't even have 20 episodes on them. This highlights the importance of staying consistent in podcasting, which can be half the battle.

In this chapter, we will explore the reasons why staying consistent in podcasting is challenging and how it is easier to stay consistent on other platforms like YouTube or Instagram.

## *Why Staying Consistent in Podcasting is Difficult?*

- Time-Consuming: Podcasting is a time-consuming process. From ideation to post-production, every aspect of podcasting requires considerable time and effort.
- Limited Feedback: Podcasts have limited feedback mechanisms, unlike other social media platforms. It is difficult to gauge how well your podcast is performing, and whether or not you are on the right track.
- High Dropout Rates: Most podcasters quit after a few episodes due to a lack of traction, limited engagement, or personal reasons.
- Technical Challenges: Podcasting involves technical skills, such as editing, mixing, and mastering, which can be challenging for beginners.

## *Why it's Easier to Stay Consistent on YouTube or Instagram?*

- Immediate Feedback: YouTube and Instagram provide immediate feedback mechanisms, such as likes, comments, and shares, which give creators an instant indication of how well their content is performing.
- Short-form Content: YouTube and Instagram have short-form content, which means that creators can create and post content quickly without spending too much time on post-production.
- High Engagement: YouTube and Instagram have a high engagement rate, which means that creators can

connect with their audience quickly and build a community around their content.

## *Why Consistency is Key in Podcasting?*

Staying consistent in podcasting is half the battle. Consistency builds trust with your audience, establishes credibility, and helps you stay relevant in the competitive world of podcasting. Here are some reasons why consistency is key in podcasting:

- Builds Momentum: Consistency builds momentum and helps you stay on track with your goals. It creates a habit and ensures that you keep moving forward.
- Increases Engagement: Consistency increases engagement with your audience. Your listeners will know when to expect new episodes, and they will be more likely to tune in regularly.
- Builds a Brand: Consistency builds a brand around your podcast. It establishes your voice, tone, and style, which helps you stand out in a crowded market.

## *Conclusion*

Staying consistent in podcasting is half the battle. However, it's easier said than done. Podcasting is a time-consuming and technical process, and staying consistent is difficult without immediate feedback mechanisms. It's easier to stay consistent on platforms like YouTube or Instagram, which provide immediate feedback and have short-form content.

Nonetheless, consistency is key in podcasting. It builds momentum, increases engagement, and helps you build a brand around your podcast.

# FIVE

# Why All Podcasters Are Storytellers?

Welcome to the world of podcasting, where you have the power to tell stories and share ideas with millions of people around the world. As a podcaster, you are not just someone who creates audio content. You are a storyteller, and storytelling is an essential part of Indian culture.

India is a land of storytellers, with a rich history of oral traditions. From the ancient epics of the Mahabharata and the Ramayana to modern-day Bollywood movies, Indian culture has always valued the power of storytelling. Podcasting is the latest medium through which Indians tell their stories and share their ideas.

In this chapter, we will explore why all podcasters are storytellers and why storytelling is an essential component of successful podcasts.

## *What is Storytelling?*

Storytelling is the art of conveying a message or idea through a narrative. A good story has the power to captivate an audience, engage their emotions, and leave a lasting impression. Whether it is a story of love, adventure, or self-discovery, storytelling has been used for centuries to communicate ideas and inspire change.

## *Podcasting and Storytelling*

Podcasting is the perfect medium for storytelling. Unlike traditional media, podcasting allows you to connect with your audience on a personal level. Listeners can hear your voice, feel your passion, and connect with your message in an impossible way with text-based media.

A podcast is a conversation between you and your listeners. Through your stories, you can connect with your audience, build trust, and establish a relationship that goes beyond the audio content.

Whether you are creating a podcast about history, food, or personal development, storytelling is an essential component of a successful podcast. Your stories are what will keep your audience engaged, interested, and coming back for more.

## *Tips for Effective Storytelling in Podcasting*

- Know Your Audience: Understanding your audience is the key to effective storytelling. You need to know what resonates with them, what interests them, and what problems they are trying to solve.

- Be Authentic: Your listeners want to hear your authentic voice. Be yourself, share your experiences, and don't fear showing your vulnerabilities.
- Keep It Simple: A good story doesn't have to be complicated. Keep your narrative simple, concise, and easy to follow.
- Use Emotion: Emotions are what make stories memorable. Use emotions to connect with your listeners and make them feel something.

## *Conclusion*

As a podcaster, you are a storyteller. Storytelling is an essential component of successful podcasts, and it is deeply ingrained in Indian culture. Whether you are sharing your personal experiences or discussing a complex topic, storytelling is what will make your podcast stand out.

# SIX

# CHOOSING THE RIGHT PODCAST TOPIC

Choosing the right topic for your podcast is critical for its success. It should be something you are passionate about, but it should also have a potential audience. In this chapter, we will discuss the factors to consider when choosing a podcast topic.

## *Passion vs. Potential Audience*

Your podcast topic should be something you are passionate about because you will be spending a lot of time talking about it.

However, you also need to consider whether there is a potential audience for your topic. If there is no audience, your podcast will not succeed.

To find out if there is an audience for your topic, do some research. Look at what other podcasts are doing in your niche, and see if they have a substantial following.

### *Niche vs. Broad Topics*

Niche topics are more specific and focused on a particular area. They have a smaller audience, but the listeners are more passionate about the topic.

Broad topics cover a larger area and have a broader audience. The competition in broad topics is high, and it's more challenging to stand out.

When choosing between a niche or a broad topic, consider your goals for the podcast. If you want to build a large following quickly, go for a broad topic. If you want a more loyal and passionate audience, go for a niche topic.

### *Originality vs. Repetition*

Your podcast topic should be original and offer something new to the audience. If you are doing the same thing as other podcasts, there is no reason for people to listen to you.

However, don't be afraid to tackle a topic that has been done before. If you have a unique perspective or approach, you can still make your podcast stand out.

### *Your Expertise*

You should choose a podcast topic that aligns with your expertise. It's easier to talk about something you know well and have experience in.

If you choose a topic that you have no experience in, you'll have to spend a lot of time researching, which can lead to burnout.

## *Evergreen vs. Timely Topics*

Evergreen topics are always relevant and have a longer shelf life. They can be listened to at any time.

Timely topics are relevant for a specific period, like news or current events. They have a short shelf life but can generate a lot of buzz.

Consider your goals for the podcast and your audience when choosing between evergreen and timely topics.

Choosing the right topic for your podcast is crucial. It should align with your passion, expertise, and potential audience. Do your research, be original, and consider your goals for the podcast to make it a success.

# SEVEN

# Creating Your Perfect Podcast Listener Avatar

When starting a podcast, it's important to have a clear understanding of who your target audience is. Your audience is the driving force behind your podcast's success, and creating a listener avatar can help you understand and cater to their needs. In this chapter, we'll explore the importance of creating a perfect podcast listener avatar and how to go about doing it.

## *What is a Perfect Podcast Listener Avatar?*

A podcast listener avatar is a detailed description of your ideal listener. It's a representation of your target audience, and it includes specific details about who they are, what they like, and what they need. A perfect podcast listener avatar is a detailed profile of one individual person that represents your entire target audience.

## *Why is it Important to Create a Perfect Podcast Listener Avatar?*

Creating a perfect podcast listener avatar can help you understand your audience better, which can help you create more engaging and relevant content. Here are some reasons why it's important to create a perfect podcast listener avatar:

- Helps you understand your audience's needs and wants
- Helps you create content that resonates with your audience
- Helps you tailor your marketing efforts to your audience
- Helps you grow your audience by creating content that attracts new listeners

## *How to Create a Perfect Podcast Listener Avatar?*

Creating a perfect podcast listener avatar requires some research and imagination. Here are some steps you can take to create a perfect podcast listener avatar:

- Research your target audience: Use analytics tools to gather data about your current listeners. Analyze their demographics, listening habits, and preferences.
- Identify their pain points: Think about the problems your audience is facing that your podcast can help solve. Identify their needs, wants, and desires.

- Develop a detailed profile: Use the data you've gathered to create a detailed profile of your ideal listener. Include details like age, gender, occupation, education, interests, and hobbies.
- Personalize your avatar: Give your avatar a name and a backstory. Make it a real person that you can relate to.

## *How to Use Your Perfect Podcast Listener Avatar?*

Once you have created a perfect podcast listener avatar, you can use it in various ways to improve your podcast. Here are some ways to use your perfect podcast listener avatar:

- Content creation: Create content that speaks directly to your perfect podcast listener avatar. This will help you create content that resonates with your target audience.
- Marketing: Use your perfect podcast listener avatar to target your marketing efforts. This will help you attract more listeners that match your avatar's profile.
- Guest selection: Use your perfect podcast listener avatar to select guests for your show. This will help you attract guests that appeal to your target audience.

In conclusion, creating a perfect podcast listener avatar is an essential step in launching and growing your podcast. It helps you understand your audience's needs and wants, and it enables you to create content that resonates with your target audience. Use the steps outlined in this chapter to create a perfect podcast listener avatar, and watch your podcast grow.

# EIGHT

# NAMING YOUR PODCAST

Your podcast's name is the first thing that potential listeners will see and hear, and it can have a significant impact on whether or not they decide to give your show a listen. In this chapter, we'll go over some tips and strategies for choosing the perfect name for your podcast.

### *Keep it Simple and Memorable*

Your podcast's name should be easy to remember and easy to spell. Avoid using overly complicated or lengthy names that are hard to remember or spell. Instead, opt for something short, catchy, and easy to pronounce. A simple, memorable name can also help your podcast stand out from the competition.

### *Make it Relevant*

Your podcast's name should give potential listeners an idea of what your show is about. This doesn't mean that you have to be overly specific or literal, but it does mean that your name should be relevant to the content of your podcast. For example, if you're starting a podcast about entrepreneurship, you might choose a name like "The Startup Mindset" or "Entrepreneurial Insights".

### *Consider SEO*

Search engine optimization (SEO) is the practice of optimizing your content to rank higher in search engine results. When choosing a name for your podcast, consider using relevant keywords that people might search for. For example, if you're starting a podcast about yoga, you might consider a name like "Yoga Flow with [Your Name]".

### *Brainstorm with Others*

Brainstorming with others can be a great way to come up with a name for your podcast. This can include friends, family members, or even your social media followers. Gather feedback and ideas from others and use them to help you come up with the perfect name for your show.

### *Check Availability*

Before you settle on a name for your podcast, make sure that it's not already in use. Check popular podcast directories like Apple Podcasts, Spotify, and Google Podcasts to see if any other shows are using the same name. You should also check to see if the domain name is available, as you'll likely want to create a website for your podcast.

### *Be Unique*

Finally, try to choose a name that is unique and stands out from the competition. Avoid using generic or cliché names that could apply to any podcast. Your name should be distinct and memorable, helping your podcast to make a lasting impression on listeners.

Naming your podcast is an important decision, so take your time and make sure that you choose a name that accurately reflects the content of your show and resonates with your target audience.

# NINE

# Understanding Your Podcast's Unique Selling Proposition (USP)

When it comes to creating a successful podcast, having a clear understanding of your show's Unique Selling Proposition (USP) is crucial. Your USP is what sets your podcast apart from others and helps attract and retain listeners. In this chapter, we will explore the importance of identifying your podcast's USP and how to do it effectively.

## *What is a Unique Selling Proposition (USP)?*

A Unique Selling Proposition (USP) is the factor that sets your podcast apart from others in your niche or category. It's the reason why listeners should choose your podcast over others. A USP should be clear, concise, and easy to communicate to potential listeners. It should answer the question: "What makes your podcast unique?"

## *Why is a USP important for your podcast?*

Having a clear USP is essential for a successful podcast for the following reasons:

- Attracting new listeners: A clear USP helps to attract new listeners who are interested in your podcast's topic and unique angle.
- Retaining listeners: Your USP also helps retain your current listeners by delivering what they expect from your podcast and differentiating your show from others.
- Monetization opportunities: A unique selling proposition also makes it easier to monetize your podcast through sponsorships, merchandise sales, and other revenue streams.

## *How to Identify Your Podcast's USP?*

Here are some steps to help you identify your podcast's unique selling proposition:

- Define your podcast's topic and target audience: Define the main topic of your podcast and identify who your ideal listener is.

- Research your competition: Look at other podcasts in your niche or category and identify what they are offering to their audience. This will help you find gaps or opportunities that you can address with your unique angle.
- Identify your unique angle: Based on your research, think about what makes your podcast different from others in your niche. Is it your storytelling style, your guests, your expertise, or your approach to the topic?
- Refine your USP: Once you have identified your unique angle, refine your USP to make it clear and easy to communicate to potential listeners. Keep in mind that your USP should be specific and not too broad.

### *Examples of Podcast USPs*

Here are some examples of podcast USPs:

- Serial: This true-crime podcast stands out for its unique storytelling style that unfolds a story over several episodes, keeping listeners hooked.
- Stuff You Should Know: This podcast stands out for its approachable and entertaining way of presenting complex topics.
- The Tim Ferriss Show: This podcast is known for its in-depth interviews with high achievers and experts in various fields, providing insights and inspiration to listeners.

### *Conclusion*

Understanding your podcast's unique selling proposition is crucial for attracting and retaining listeners and monetizing your show. By following the steps outlined in this chapter, you can identify your USP and create a podcast that stands out in your niche or category.

# TEN

# THE IMPORTANCE OF PODCAST INTRO

An engaging podcast intro can help you hook your listeners and keep them coming back for more. In this chapter, we will discuss the importance of a podcast intro and how you can create one that grabs your listeners' attention.

### *The First Impression Matters*

Your podcast intro is the first thing your listeners hear, and it sets the tone for the entire show.

A well-crafted intro can leave a lasting impression on your listeners and make them excited for what's to come.

### *Establishing Your Brand*

Your podcast intro can help establish your brand and give your show a unique identity.

By using music, sound effects, and a distinctive voiceover, you can create an intro that reflects your podcast's personality and style.

### *Setting Expectations*

Your podcast intro can also set expectations for your listeners.

By introducing your topic or theme, you can give your listeners an idea of what they can expect from the show.

This can help attract the right audience and keep them engaged.

### *Grabbing Attention*

Your podcast intro needs to grab your listener's attention and make them want to keep listening.

You can do this by using a catchy hook, an intriguing story, or an interesting fact.

Make sure your intro is concise and to the point, so you don't lose your listener's interest.

### *Adding Production Value*

A well-produced podcast intro can add production value to your show.

By using music, sound effects, and professional voiceover talent, you can create an intro that sounds polished and professional.

This can help build credibility and make your show stand out.

## *Consistency*

Your podcast intro should be consistent across all episodes.

This will help establish your brand and make it easier for your listeners to recognize your show.

Consistency also helps create a sense of familiarity and comfort for your listeners.

## *Call to Action*

Your podcast intro is also an opportunity to include a call to action.

You can encourage your listeners to subscribe, leave a review, or visit your website.

This can help grow your audience and increase engagement.

In conclusion, a well-crafted podcast intro is essential to the success of your show. It sets the tone, establishes your brand, and grabs your listener's attention. With the right approach, you can create an intro that keeps your listeners coming back for more.

# ELEVEN

# YOUR PODCAST'S VISUAL IDENTITY

Your podcast channel art and episode art are critical components of your podcast's visual identity. They are the first things that potential listeners see when they come across your podcast, and they can make a big difference in whether or not someone decides to listen. In this chapter, we'll discuss why podcast channel art and episode art are so important, what they should look like, and how to create them.

## *The Importance of Podcast Channel Art*

Your podcast channel art is the image that appears at the top of your podcast page on various streaming platforms, such as Apple Podcasts, Spotify, and Google Podcasts. It's essentially your podcast's logo and should be eye-catching and memorable. Here's why it's important:

- It makes a first impression: As we mentioned earlier, your podcast channel art is the first thing that potential

listeners see when they come across your podcast. If it doesn't stand out or if it looks unprofessional, they might not give your podcast a chance.
- It reflects your brand: Your podcast channel art should be a reflection of your podcast's brand. If you have a comedy podcast, for example, your channel art should be fun and playful.
- It sets you apart from the competition: There are over two million podcasts out there, so it's important to make sure your podcast stands out. Having great channel art can help set you apart from your competitors.

## *What Your Podcast Channel Art Should Look Like*

Now that you understand why your podcast channel art is important, let's talk about what it should look like. Here are a few things to keep in mind:

- It should be simple: Your channel art shouldn't be too busy or cluttered. Keep it simple and easy to read.
- It should be visually appealing: Your channel art should be eye-catching and visually appealing. Use colors and imagery that will draw people in.
- It should be high quality: Make sure your channel art is high resolution so that it looks good on all devices.
- It should be consistent: Your channel art should be consistent with your podcast's brand. If you have a website or social media pages, make sure your channel art matches those designs.

## *The Importance of Episode Art*

Episode art is the image that appears next to each individual episode of your podcast. Here's why it's important:

- It helps to visually differentiate episodes: If someone is scrolling through a list of episodes, episode art can help them quickly differentiate between episodes and find the one they're looking for.
- It can be used for promotion: You can use your episode art to promote your podcast on social media or other platforms.

## *What Your Episode Art Should Look Like*

Now that you understand why episode art is important, let's talk about what it should look like. Here are a few things to keep in mind:

- It should be relevant: Your episode art should be relevant to the content of the episode.
- It should be visually appealing: Just like your channel art, your episode art should be visually appealing and eye-catching.
- It should be consistent: Try to keep your episode art consistent so that listeners can quickly recognize your podcast.

### ***How to Create Podcast Channel Art and Episode Art***

Creating podcast channel art and episode art doesn't have to be difficult or expensive. Here are a few tips for creating great art:

- Use a design tool: There are plenty of free design tools out there, such as Canva and Adobe Spark, that make it easy to create great designs.
- Hire a designer: If you're not confident in your design skills, consider hiring a designer to create

# TWELVE

# Being Tech-Savvy in Podcasting

Podcasting has become a popular medium for creators to share their ideas, opinions, and stories with the world. However, the success of a podcast relies heavily on the quality of the audio and the post-production work that goes into it. This is where being tech-savvy comes into play. In this chapter, we will explore why successful podcasters are slightly tech-savvy and the importance of befriending a tech-savvy person.

## *Why Being Tech-Savvy is Important in Podcasting?*

**Setting Up Equipment**: Setting up the equipment for podcasting can be daunting for beginners. From choosing the right microphone to setting up a recording space, many technical aspects are involved in the process.

**Post-Production Work**: Post-production work involves editing, mixing, and mastering the audio. It also includes adding sound effects, music, and intros/outros. All of these tasks require some level of technical expertise.

**Troubleshooting**: Technical issues are bound to arise during the podcasting process. Being tech-savvy can help you troubleshoot and fix these issues quickly.

**Saving Time**: Knowing how to use the technology involved in podcasting can save you a lot of time. It can help you work more efficiently, produce high-quality audio, and reduce the need for re-takes.

## *Befriending a Tech-Savvy Person*

**Learn from Them**: Befriending a tech-savvy person can help you learn the technical aspects of podcasting. They can teach you how to set up equipment, how to edit audio, and how to troubleshoot technical issues.

**Collaboration**: Befriending a tech-savvy person can also lead to collaborations. They can help you produce high-quality audio and make your podcast stand out in a crowded market.

**Saving Time**: Befriending a tech-savvy person can save you a lot of time. They can help you work more efficiently and reduce the need for re-takes.

## *Conclusion*

Being tech-savvy is essential in podcasting. Everything requires a little bit of technical expertise, from setting up equipment to post-production work. However, learning the technical aspects of podcasting can be a steep learning curve for beginners. Befriending a tech-savvy person can help you learn, collaborate, and save time. In the next chapter, we will explore the importance of choosing the right topic and format for your podcast.

# THIRTEEN

# PODCAST RSS - THE KEY TO DISTRIBUTING YOUR PODCAST

If you're planning to distribute your podcast to multiple platforms, including Apple Podcasts, Spotify, and Google Podcasts, then you'll need to know about podcast RSS. This is a technology that enables your podcast to be distributed across various podcast platforms, making it easier for listeners to find and subscribe to your show. In this chapter, we'll dive deeper into what podcast RSS is, why it's important, and how to use it to distribute your podcast.

### *What is Podcast RSS?*

Podcast RSS (Really Simple Syndication) is a web feed that contains all the information about your podcast, including its title, description, cover art, and episode details. The RSS feed acts as a central hub for all the information about your podcast, and podcast apps like Apple Podcasts, Spotify, and Google Podcasts use this feed to display your show to listeners.

### *Why is Podcast RSS Important?*

Podcast RSS is essential because it allows your podcast to be distributed to multiple platforms, making it easier for listeners to find and subscribe to your show. By using an RSS feed, you can ensure that your podcast is accessible to listeners across all the major podcast platforms.

### *How to Create a Podcast RSS Feed?*

To create a podcast RSS feed, you'll need to use a podcast hosting service. Most hosting services like Buzzsprout, Libsyn, and Anchor provide an RSS feed automatically for your podcast. All you need to do is create an account, upload your podcast episodes, and the hosting service will generate an RSS feed for you.

### *How to Submit Your Podcast RSS Feed to Podcast Directories?*

Once you have your podcast RSS feed, you can submit it to podcast directories like Apple Podcasts, Spotify, and Google Podcasts. Each platform has its submission process, but generally, you'll need to follow these steps:

- Create an account on the podcast platform
- Find the section for submitting a new podcast
- Enter your RSS feed URL

- Wait for the platform to review and approve your podcast

## *How to Troubleshoot Podcast RSS Feed Errors?*

Sometimes, you might encounter errors with your podcast RSS feed. The most common error is a validation error, which occurs when your RSS feed doesn't meet the required format. To fix these errors, you'll need to use an RSS feed validator tool like Cast Feed Validator or W3C Feed Validation Service.

## *Conclusion:*

Podcast RSS is a crucial part of distributing your podcast to multiple platforms. By creating and submitting your RSS feed, you can make it easier for listeners to find and subscribe to your show across all the major podcast directories. If you're experiencing any issues with your RSS feed, be sure to use a validator tool to troubleshoot any errors.

# FOURTEEN

# Podcast Hosting

If you're planning to start a podcast, you'll need a reliable podcast hosting service. A hosting service is where you upload your podcast episodes and is responsible for delivering your podcast to listeners on various podcast platforms. In this chapter, we'll discuss the importance of podcast hosting and how to choose the right one for your podcast.

### *Why is podcast hosting important?*

Podcast hosting is important for the following reasons:

- Reliable hosting ensures your podcast is always available to listeners.
- Most podcast platforms require a podcast to have a hosting service.
- Hosting services provide analytics to track your podcast's performance.

- Hosting services can also help you monetize your podcast by offering sponsorships and advertising opportunities.

### *What to consider when choosing a podcast hosting service?*

When choosing a podcast hosting service, consider the following factors:

- Pricing: Look for a hosting service that offers pricing that fits your budget.
- Storage: Ensure the hosting service offers enough storage for your podcast episodes.
- Bandwidth: Make sure the hosting service offers enough bandwidth to handle the number of listeners and downloads.
- Analytics: Look for a hosting service that provides detailed analytics to track your podcast's performance.
- Integration: Choose a hosting service that integrates with popular podcast platforms.
- Support: Ensure the hosting service offers reliable support in case of technical issues.

### *Top podcast hosting services*

Here are some popular podcast hosting services to consider:

- Anchor.fm
- Buzzsprout
- Libsyn

- Podbean
- Transistor
- Blubrry
- Simplecast
- Captivate

## *How to upload your podcast to a hosting service?*

To upload your podcast to a hosting service, follow these general steps:

- Create an account with the hosting service.
- Create an RSS feed for your podcast using the hosting service's tools.
- Upload your podcast episode to the hosting service.
- Publish your podcast episode to your RSS feed.
- Submit your podcast RSS feed to popular podcast platforms like Apple Podcasts, Spotify, and Google Podcasts.

## *Conclusion*

Choosing the right podcast hosting service is essential for the success of your podcast. Consider the pricing, storage, bandwidth, analytics, integration, and support offered by hosting services before choosing one. After selecting a hosting service, upload your podcast episode and publish it to your RSS feed for distribution on popular podcast platforms.

# FIFTEEN

# PODCAST SCRIPTING

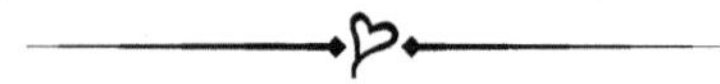

Podcast scripting involves creating a detailed plan for your podcast episode, including the structure, tone, and content of each segment. It can help you stay organized, ensure your message is clear and concise, and make your podcast more engaging for your listeners. In this chapter, we'll explore the importance of podcast scripting and provide some tips on how to create effective scripts.

### *The Importance of Podcast Scripting*

- Helps you stay organized and on track
- Ensures your message is clear and concise
- Makes your podcast more engaging for listeners

### *Tips for Creating Effective Podcast Scripts*

- Define your podcast's format and structure
- Plan out each segment of your podcast
- Use an outline to keep your thoughts organized
- Write in a conversational tone
- Use storytelling to keep your audience engaged
- Practice reading your script aloud to refine your delivery
- Leave room for ad-libs and improvisation

## *Tools for Podcast Scripting*

- Writing software like Google Docs or Microsoft Word
- Podcast scripting templates
- Mind mapping tools like MindMeister or Coggle

## *Common Podcast Scripting Mistakes*

- Over-scripting can make your podcast sound robotic or unnatural
- Lack of preparation can lead to rambling or unfocused episodes
- Ignoring audience engagement can result in a disinterested audience
- Failing to adapt to changes in your podcast's structure or format

By following these tips and avoiding common mistakes, you can create effective podcast scripts that engage your audience and deliver your message in a clear and concise manner.

# SIXTEEN

# Podcast Directories: How to Get Your Podcast Found

Podcast directories are the primary source of discovery for many listeners. While there are many ways to promote your podcast, being listed in the right directories can make all the difference. In this chapter, we'll discuss what podcast directories are and how to get your podcast listed in them.

### ***What are podcast directories?***

Podcast directories are online platforms that allow users to find and listen to podcasts. They are essentially search engines for podcasts. There are several popular podcast directories, including Apple Podcasts, Spotify, Google Podcasts, Stitcher, and TuneIn.

## *Why are podcast directories important?*

Podcast directories are essential for the discovery of new podcasts. Listeners often use directories to find and subscribe to new shows. Being listed in popular directories can help increase your visibility and attract new listeners. Additionally, many directories offer features such as ratings and reviews, which can help establish credibility and build your audience.

## *How to get your podcast listed in directories?*

To get your podcast listed in directories, you first need to create an RSS feed for your show. An RSS feed is a file that contains all of your podcast episodes and metadata. Most podcast hosting platforms, such as Buzzsprout, Libsyn, and Podbean, automatically generate an RSS feed for you.

Once you have an RSS feed, you can submit it to various podcast directories. Each directory has its submission process, but most require you to provide your RSS feed URL and some basic information about your show.

Here are the submission links for some of the most popular podcast directories:

- Apple Podcasts: https://podcastsconnect.apple.com/
- Spotify: https://podcasters.spotify.com/
- Google Podcasts: https://podcastsmanager.google.com/about
- Stitcher: https://www.stitcher.com/content-providers

- TuneIn: https://help.tunein.com/contact/add-podcast-S1l5nwTWX

## *Best practices for podcast directory submissions*

When submitting your podcast to directories, there are a few best practices to keep in mind:

- Ensure that your podcast meets the directory's technical requirements, such as file format and size limits.
- Use clear and descriptive titles and descriptions to help users understand what your show is about.
- Include relevant keywords in your title and description to improve your search rankings.
- Use eye-catching artwork that stands out in directory listings.
- Encourage your listeners to rate and review your show on directory platforms to improve your visibility and credibility.

In conclusion, podcast directories are a crucial tool for podcast discovery and can help increase your visibility and attract new listeners. By following best practices and submitting your podcast to popular directories, you can maximize your show's exposure and build a loyal audience.

# SEVENTEEN

# PODCAST NARRATION TECHNIQUES AND STYLES

Podcast narration is an essential element of any successful podcast. It sets the tone, conveys information, and engages your audience. There are several different narration techniques and styles to choose from, each with its own benefits and drawbacks. In this chapter, we'll explore some of the most popular techniques and styles for podcast narration.

## *Scripted Narration*

Scripted narration involves writing a complete script for your podcast episode, and then reading it verbatim. This approach is ideal for podcasts that require a high level of precision and accuracy, such as news, educational, or informative podcasts. Scripted narration ensures that you convey your message exactly as intended, and also allows for easy editing and revision.

### *Conversational Narration*

Conversational narration is a more relaxed and informal style of narration that aims to create a sense of intimacy and connection with the audience. It involves speaking in a natural tone and using everyday language, just like you would in a conversation with a friend. This approach is well-suited to podcasts that cover personal stories, interviews, or other topics that require a more informal tone.

### *Extemporaneous Narration*

Extemporaneous narration involves speaking off the cuff, without a script or notes. This style of narration can create a sense of spontaneity and authenticity, and can be especially effective in podcasts that cover breaking news, events, or other time-sensitive topics. However, it can also be challenging to maintain coherence and structure without a script or outline.

### *Storytelling Narration*

Storytelling narration is a style of podcasting that uses narrative techniques to create a compelling story or series of stories. This approach can be highly engaging and memorable, and is well-suited to podcasts that cover history, true crime, or other narrative-driven topics. However, it can also require more planning and preparation than other narration styles, as you'll need to develop a clear storyline and structure.

### *Dramatic Narration*

Dramatic narration involves using vocal inflection, pacing, and other techniques to create a dramatic or suspenseful effect. This approach can be highly effective in podcasts that cover horror, science fiction, or other genres that require a sense of tension and suspense. However, it can also be challenging to maintain this style over the course of an entire podcast episode without becoming monotonous or overwrought.

### *Conclusion:*

Ultimately, the best narration style for your podcast will depend on your topic, audience, and personal preferences. Experiment with different techniques and styles to find the one that works best for you and your podcast. Remember that effective narration is essential to engaging your audience and keeping them coming back for more.

# EIGHTEEN

# PROMOTE YOUR PODCAST

One of the most crucial aspects of podcasting is promoting your content to reach a wider audience. Here are some effective strategies to promote your podcast:

### *Optimize Your Podcast for Search Engines*

It's important to make your podcast easily discoverable by search engines. Optimize your podcast title, and description, and show notes with relevant keywords to improve your chances of being found by potential listeners.

### *Leverage Social Media*

Social media platforms such as Facebook, Twitter, Instagram, and LinkedIn are powerful tools for promoting your podcast. Share new episodes, behind-the-scenes photos, and updates on your social media accounts. Encourage your listeners to share your content on their own social media accounts.

### *Cross-Promotion*

Partnering with other podcasters in your niche can help you reach new listeners. Consider doing guest spots on other podcasts, and in turn, invite other podcasters to be guests on your show.

### *Build an Email List*

Building an email list is a great way to stay in touch with your listeners and promote your podcast. Offer exclusive content or early access to new episodes in exchange for their email address.

### *Attend Podcasting Conferences*

Attending podcasting conferences is a great way to network with other podcasters, learn new skills, and promote your podcast to a wider audience.

### *Create a Website*

Having a dedicated website for your podcast can help establish your brand and make it easier for listeners to find your content. Include links to your podcast on your website, as well as show notes, bios of your hosts, and other relevant information.

### *Advertise Your Podcast*

Advertising your podcast on platforms such as Facebook, Instagram, and Google Ads can help you reach a wider audience. Consider targeting audiences that are interested in your podcast's niche.

### *Use Paid Promotion*

Platforms like Apple Podcasts, Spotify, and other podcast directories offer paid promotion options that can help increase your visibility and reach.

Remember, promoting your podcast is an ongoing process. Continuously look for new ways to reach your target audience and engage with your listeners to keep them coming back for more.

# NINETEEN

# FINDING PODCAST EPISODE IDEAS

As a podcaster, it's essential to come up with fresh and exciting ideas for your podcast episodes. The content of your podcast is what will keep your audience engaged and coming back for more. In this chapter, we will explore different techniques and approaches for finding podcast episode ideas.

## *Brainstorming*

The first step to finding podcast episode ideas is to brainstorm. Sit down and think about what your podcast is about, who your target audience is, and what topics interest them. Make a list of broad topics and then narrow them down to more specific ideas. Try to come up with as many ideas as possible, and don't be afraid to be creative.

### *Social Media*

Social media can be a great source of inspiration for podcast episode ideas. Follow people in your industry or niche and pay attention to the conversations they're having. Look for trending topics or discussions that are getting a lot of attention. You can also ask your followers for suggestions on what they would like to hear on your podcast.

### *News and Current Events*

Current events can be a great source of inspiration for podcast episodes. Keep an eye on the news and look for stories or events that are relevant to your podcast's topic. You can also tie in your personal experiences and perspectives on these events to make your podcast more unique.

### *Interviews*

Interviewing guests can be a great way to come up with new podcast episode ideas. Ask your guests about their experiences and perspectives on different topics, and use their responses as inspiration for future episodes.

### *Audience Feedback*

Pay attention to your audience's feedback and comments. Look for common themes or questions that they have and use them as inspiration for new episodes. You can also create listener surveys or polls to gather more specific feedback on what your audience wants to hear.

### *Repurposing Content*

If you have a blog or another content platform, you can repurpose that content into podcast episodes. Look for blog posts or articles that have performed well and turn them into podcast episodes. This is a great way to reach a new audience and give your existing content a new life.

In conclusion, finding podcast episode ideas requires creativity, research, and understanding your audience. By using these techniques and approaches, you can come up with fresh and exciting ideas that will keep your audience engaged and coming back for more.

# TWENTY
# PODCAST DISCOVERABILITY

In today's world, creating great content is not enough to get your podcast noticed. To stand out in a crowded market, you need to make your podcast discoverable to your potential listeners. This is where Podcast SEO comes into play. In this chapter, we will discuss the importance of Podcast SEO and the steps you can take to optimize your podcast for search engines and directories.

## *What is Podcast SEO?*

Podcast SEO is the process of optimizing your podcast to rank higher in search engines and directories such as Apple Podcasts, Spotify, and Google Podcasts. This process involves optimizing various elements of your podcast, including titles, descriptions, tags, and audio content, to increase its visibility and reach.

## *Why is Podcast SEO important?*

Podcast SEO is important because it helps your podcast get discovered by a wider audience. By optimizing your podcast for search engines and directories, you can increase your visibility and reach, which can lead to more subscribers, downloads, and ultimately more revenue.

## *How to optimize your Podcast for SEO?*

- Optimize Your Podcast Title: Your podcast title is the first thing that potential listeners will see, so it's important to make it compelling and descriptive. Make sure to include relevant keywords in your title to help search engines and directories understand what your podcast is about.
- Write a Clear and Compelling Description: Your podcast description should provide a clear and compelling overview of what your podcast is about. Make sure to include relevant keywords and phrases that describe your podcast's topic and theme.
- Use Relevant Keywords and Phrases: Keywords and phrases are essential for helping search engines and directories understand what your podcast is about. Make sure to include relevant keywords and phrases in your podcast title, description, and tags.
- Include ID3 Tags: ID3 tags are metadata tags that are embedded in your audio file. These tags help search engines and directories understand what your podcast is about, and they also provide additional information such as the episode title, description, and artwork.
- Promote Your Podcast: Promoting your podcast on social media and other channels can help increase your podcast's visibility and reach. The more exposure your

podcast gets, the more likely it is to be discovered by potential listeners.

## ***Benefits of Podcast SEO***

- Increased Visibility: Optimizing your podcast for search engines and directories can increase its visibility and reach.
- More Subscribers and Downloads: The more visible your podcast is, the more likely it is to attract new subscribers and downloads.
- Higher Rankings: By optimizing your podcast for search engines, you can improve its ranking and increase its chances of being discovered by potential listeners.
- More Revenue: With more subscribers and downloads, you can monetize your podcast through sponsorships, ads, and other revenue streams.

In conclusion, Podcast SEO is essential for making your podcast discoverable to potential listeners. By following the steps outlined in this chapter, you can optimize your podcast for search engines and directories and increase its visibility and reach. Remember, great content is only one part of the equation. To be successful, you need to make sure your podcast is discoverable and accessible to your audience.

# TWENTY-ONE

# Being Persuasive in Podcasting

Podcasting has become a popular medium for creators to promote their businesses or affiliate products. However, the success of these promotional efforts relies heavily on the creator's ability to persuade their listeners to take action. In this chapter, we will explore why being persuasive is essential in podcasting and how it can help you make money.

### *Why Being Persuasive is Important in Podcasting?*

- Promoting Your Business or Affiliate Products: If you're using your podcast to promote your business or affiliate products, you need to persuade your listeners to buy from you. You need to convince them that your product or service is worth their time and money.

- Pitching Sponsors: If you're pitching sponsors for your podcast, you need to persuade them to say yes to your ask. You need to convince them that your podcast is worth investing in and that their brand will benefit from the exposure.
- Retaining Listeners: Even getting a normal listener to listen to your episode till the end will require you to be persuasive. You need to convince them that your content is worth their time and that they should keep listening.

## *How to Be Persuasive in Podcasting?*

- Know Your Audience: Understanding your audience is crucial when it comes to being persuasive. You need to know their needs, wants, and pain points to create content that resonates with them.
- Use Storytelling: Storytelling is a powerful tool for persuasion. It can help you connect with your audience on an emotional level and make them more receptive to your message.
- Use Social Proof: Social proof is the idea that people are more likely to take action if they see others doing it first. You can use social proof in your podcast by sharing testimonials, reviews, or success stories from your customers or listeners.
- Call to Action: A call to action is a statement that encourages your audience to take action. It could be as simple as asking them to subscribe to your podcast, leave a review, or buy your product.

## *Conclusion*

Being persuasive is crucial in podcasting if you want to make money. Whether you're promoting your business or affiliate products, pitching sponsors, or retaining listeners, being persuasive can help you achieve your goals. To be persuasive, you need to know your audience, use storytelling, social proof, and calls to action.

# TWENTY-TWO
# The Importance of Networking in Podcasting

Networking is a critical component of any successful podcasting venture. It can help you gain exposure, connect with potential sponsors, and even land exclusive deals with major streaming platforms like Spotify. In this chapter, we will explore why networking is so important and provide some tips on how to make the most of your networking efforts.

## *Leveraging Your Network*

Networking isn't just about attending events and shaking hands. It's about leveraging the relationships you already have to create new opportunities. Start by reaching out to your friends, family, and colleagues to see if they have any connections in the podcasting industry. You never know who might be able to introduce you to a potential sponsor or help you land an exclusive deal with a major streaming platform.

## *Building Relationships*

Networking is all about building relationships. This means taking the time to get to know people, understanding their needs, and finding ways to provide value to them. Attend events and conferences, join online groups and forums, and participate in social media conversations. The more you put yourself out there and engage with others, the more likely you are to build meaningful relationships.

## *Collaboration, Not Competition*

One of the biggest mistakes people make when networking is thinking of others as competition. In reality, there is room for everyone in the podcasting industry. Collaborate with other podcasters in your niche, offer to promote each other's shows, and even consider co-hosting an episode together. This can help you expand your audience and create valuable relationships that can lead to future opportunities.

## *Giving Before Receiving*

Networking is not just about asking for favours. It's about giving before you receive. Offer to help other podcasters with their projects, share your expertise, and provide value to your network in any way you can. This will help you build trust and establish yourself as a valuable member of the community.

## *Follow Up*

Finally, don't forget to follow up with your network. After attending an event or meeting someone new, send a follow-up email or message to thank them for their time and reiterate any action items or next steps. This will help you stay top of mind and ensure that your networking efforts don't go to waste.

## *Conclusion:*

Networking is a critical component of any successful podcasting venture. By leveraging your network, building relationships, collaborating with others, giving before receiving, and following up, you can create valuable opportunities and take your podcast to the next level. So, start putting yourself out there and see where your networking efforts can take you!

# TWENTY-THREE

# Avoiding Copyright Strikes in Podcasting

Podcasting is a great platform for sharing your ideas and creativity with the world, but it's important to make sure that you're not infringing on anyone else's copyright while doing so.

### *Understanding Copyright Laws*

Copyright laws vary from country to country, but generally, it protects the original works of authors, composers, and artists. These works can include music, videos, images, and written content. As a podcaster, it's important to understand what you can and can't use in your podcast without getting into legal trouble.

### *Getting Permission*

If you want to use copyrighted material in your podcast, the best way to avoid any potential legal issues is to obtain permission from the copyright owner. This can include contacting the artist or record label directly, or using a licensing service such as Soundstripe or Epidemic Sound. Keep in mind that some artists and labels may require payment in exchange for permission to use their music.

### *Using Royalty-Free Music*

Another option for podcasters is to use royalty-free music. This type of music is typically available for free or for a fee, and can be used in your podcast without worrying about copyright strikes. Some popular sources of royalty-free music include YouTube's Audio Library, Free Music Archive, and PremiumBeat.

### *Creating Your Own Music*

If you have a musical talent, you can create your own music for your podcast. This not only avoids any copyright issues, but also adds a unique touch to your podcast. There are many digital audio workstations available such as Logic Pro, Ableton Live, and FL Studio that can help you create your own music.

### *Using Public Domain Material*

Public domain material includes works whose copyright has expired, such as old classical music and literature. These works can be used freely in your podcast without worrying about copyright strikes. However, it's important to make sure that the material you're using is actually in the public domain before using it.

## *Conclusion*

Copyright strikes can be a nightmare for podcasters, but with a little bit of knowledge and planning, you can avoid them altogether. Always make sure to get permission or use royalty-free music, create your own music or use public domain material. By doing so, you can keep your podcast running smoothly without worrying about legal issues.

# TWENTY-FOUR

# Choosing the Right Microphone for Your Podcast

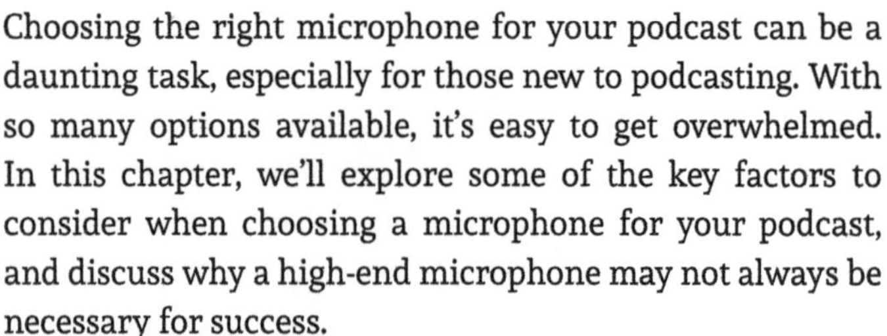

Choosing the right microphone for your podcast can be a daunting task, especially for those new to podcasting. With so many options available, it's easy to get overwhelmed. In this chapter, we'll explore some of the key factors to consider when choosing a microphone for your podcast, and discuss why a high-end microphone may not always be necessary for success.

## *Understanding Microphone Types*

There are three main types of microphones used in podcasting: dynamic, condenser, and ribbon. Dynamic microphones are durable and great for recording in noisy environments, while condenser microphones are more sensitive and ideal for capturing subtle nuances in sound. Ribbon microphones are less common but are known for their warm, vintage sound.

## *The Importance of Sound Quality*

Good sound quality is essential for a successful podcast. Your listeners want to be able to hear you clearly and without any distracting background noise. While a high-end microphone can certainly help improve your sound quality, it's not always necessary. Many successful podcasters use affordable microphones and still produce great-sounding content.

## *Cost vs. Quality*

It's easy to assume that a more expensive microphone is always better, but that's not necessarily the case. In fact, the most important factor in choosing a microphone is how well it complements your voice and the overall tone of your podcast. It's possible to find a great microphone at a reasonable price, and sometimes, a cheaper microphone can actually produce better results than a more expensive one.

## *Our Experience with Microphones*

At Ghost Stories in Hindi, we use a cheap lavalier microphone and have found great success with it. We did experiment with a high-end microphone at one point, but our audience didn't like the texture it produced. It's important to remember that what works for one podcast may not work for another, and that it's ultimately up to you to decide what microphone is best for your needs.

In conclusion, choosing the right microphone for your podcast is an important decision that can have a big impact on the quality of your content. While a high-end microphone can certainly help improve your sound quality, it's not always necessary. The most important factor is how well the microphone complements your voice and the overall tone of your podcast. By understanding the different types of microphones and considering your budget, you can choose a microphone that's perfect for your needs.

# TWENTY-FIVE

# OTHER PODCASTING GEARS

When it comes to podcasting, having good audio quality is essential. While having a good microphone is important, there are also other additional podcasting gears that can help improve your audio quality and overall production value. In this chapter, we'll explore some of the additional podcasting gears you can consider investing in to take your podcast to the next level.

### *Ring Light/Soft Box*

One of the essential podcasting gears is a ring light or soft box. These devices can help to evenly light your face and make you look more professional during video podcasting. Ring lights are particularly useful for creating a "catch light" in your eyes, which can help make your eyes appear brighter and more engaging. Soft boxes are great for diffusing light and creating an even, natural-looking light source. Investing in a ring light or soft box can help improve the visual quality of your podcast.

### *Microphone Stand*

A microphone stand is a useful addition to any podcasting setup. It allows you to position your microphone exactly where you need it and keep it steady throughout the recording. This can help you maintain a consistent audio quality throughout the podcast. It also frees up your hands to allow for more natural gestures and movements.

### *Pop Filter*

A pop filter is another important accessory that can help to improve your audio quality. It helps to reduce popping sounds caused by plosives, such as the letters "p" and "b" when speaking into the microphone. This can make your audio sound smoother and more professional. Pop filters are easy to install and are often inexpensive, making them a worthwhile investment.

### *Headphones*

Wearing headphones during podcast recording is important to ensure that you are hearing the audio as it is being recorded. It helps you to monitor the audio quality and pick up on any issues that may need to be addressed during the recording. Wearing headphones also helps to eliminate external noise and feedback, ensuring a clear and consistent audio recording.

### *Audio Interface*

An audio interface is a device that connects your microphone to your computer and allows you to adjust the audio settings, such as gain, volume, and EQ. It can help improve the overall audio quality of your podcast by giving you more control over the recording process. Some audio interfaces also come with built-in effects such as compression and reverb, which can add depth and warmth to your recordings.

### *Conclusion*

Incorporating these additional podcasting gears can help to improve the audio and visual quality of your podcast, making it more professional and engaging. Investing in these accessories may require some initial costs, but the benefits they provide can make a significant difference in the overall success of your podcast. So, consider adding these podcasting gears to your setup and take your podcast to the next level.

# TWENTY-SIX

# Best Audio Interface for Podcasting

If you're looking to improve the audio quality of your podcast, investing in an audio interface can be a great way to go. Here are some of the top audio interfaces on the market for podcasters:

### *Focusrite Scarlett 2i2*

The Focusrite Scarlett 2i2 is a popular choice for podcasters due to its affordability, simplicity, and high-quality audio. It features two XLR inputs, two 1/4 inch inputs, and 24-bit/192kHz recording capabilities. Plus, its compact size makes it easy to transport for remote recording sessions.

### *PreSonus AudioBox USB 96*

The PreSonus AudioBox USB 96 is another affordable option for podcasters. It features two combo XLR/1/4 inch inputs, 24-bit/96kHz recording capabilities, and comes with PreSonus' Studio One Artist DAW software. The AudioBox USB 96 also includes a headphone output with level control and phantom power for condenser microphones.

### *Universal Audio Apollo Twin X*

The Universal Audio Apollo Twin X is a high-end audio interface that offers exceptional audio quality and processing power. It features two XLR/1/4 inch combo inputs, two line outputs, and 24-bit/192kHz recording capabilities. The Apollo Twin X also includes built-in UAD-2 processing, allowing for real-time processing of effects and plugins.

### *Zoom H6*

The Zoom H6 is a portable recorder that can also function as an audio interface. It features four XLR inputs, two 1/4 inch inputs, and can record up to six tracks simultaneously. The H6 also includes a built-in stereo microphone, making it a versatile option for on-the-go recording.

### *Rode AI-1*

The Rode AI-1 is a simple and affordable audio interface designed specifically for podcasters and content creators. It features a single XLR input, a headphone output with level control, and 24-bit/96kHz recording capabilities. The AI-1 also includes a free copy of Rode's recording software, Ableton Live Lite.

## *Conclusion*

Choosing the right audio interface for your podcast depends on your specific needs and budget. Whether you're just starting out or looking to upgrade your equipment, any of the audio interfaces mentioned in this chapter can help you achieve high-quality sound for your podcast.

# TWENTY-SEVEN

# SELECTING THE RIGHT DIGITAL AUDIO WORKSTATION

When it comes to producing a podcast, recording and editing your audio is one of the most important steps in ensuring a high-quality final product. Choosing the right digital audio workstation (DAW) is essential for achieving this goal. This chapter will discuss the factors you should consider when selecting the correct DAW for your podcast post-production.

## *Understanding Your Needs*

Before selecting a DAW, you should first understand your podcast's post-production needs. Consider the following questions:

- What is the complexity of your podcast? Will you need to add music, sound effects, or multiple audio tracks?
- What is your budget? Do you need a free DAW or can you invest in a paid option?
- What is your experience level with audio editing software?

## *Popular DAWs for Podcasters*

There are many DAWs available on the market, but not all of them are created equal. Here are some of the most popular options for podcasters:

- Audacity: This is a free, open-source DAW that is widely used in the podcasting community. It is easy to use and has a variety of features, including noise reduction, EQ, and compression.
- Hindenburg Journalist: This DAW is designed specifically for audio journalists and podcasters. It has a clean interface and intuitive features that make editing audio simple and fast. The downside is that it is relatively expensive compared to other options.
- Reaper: This powerful DAW is great for more complex audio editing. It has a low learning curve and a customizable interface, making it a favourite among podcasters who are comfortable with audio editing software.
- Adobe Audition: This is a professional-grade DAW that is widely used in the music industry. It has powerful features that allow for complex audio editing and restoration but also has a steeper learning curve and a higher price tag.

- F L Studio: I personally use this at Ghost Stories because I learnt this software back in 2015 to produce our music videos ( as me and my sister are also singers). It is most famous among Music Producers.

## *Factors to Consider*

When selecting a DAW, there are several factors you should consider beyond just the price and features. These include:

- Compatibility: Make sure the DAW you choose is compatible with your operating system and any plugins or add-ons you plan to use.
- Support: Consider the level of support the DAW offers, including online tutorials, forums, and customer service.
- Workflow: Look for a DAW that fits your workflow and is easy to navigate. Consider the number of steps it takes to complete common tasks, and whether the DAW integrates well with other software or tools you may be using.

## *Conclusion*

Selecting the right DAW is crucial for producing a high-quality podcast. Consider your podcast's post-production needs, your budget, and your experience level when choosing a DAW. Audacity is a popular free option, while Hindenburg Journalist and Reaper are great for podcasters who need more advanced features. Finally, make sure the DAW you choose is compatible with your operating system, offers support, and fits your workflow.

# TWENTY-EIGHT

# Podcast Audio Editing

Editing audio is an essential part of podcast production. Good editing can make your podcast sound professional and polished, while poor editing can turn off listeners. In this chapter, we'll explore the different aspects of audio editing for podcasts.

### *Basic audio editing software*

There are many audio editing software options available, from free to paid. Some popular options include Audacity, GarageBand, Adobe Audition, and Hindenburg Journalist. Each software has its own unique features and interface, so it's important to choose one that suits your needs and preferences.

### *Cleaning up audio*

Once you have your audio recorded, you may need to clean up any unwanted noise, such as background hum or clicks and pops. This can be done with noise reduction tools, equalization, and compression.

### *Trimming and editing*

After cleaning up your audio, it's time to trim and edit your podcast. This involves cutting out any unnecessary pauses or sections, adding music or sound effects, and adjusting the overall volume levels.

### *Adding intros and outros*

Intros and outros are an important part of a podcast, as they set the tone and introduce the episode. It's important to make them stand out and memorable. You can create your own or use pre-made templates.

### *Mixing and mastering*

Mixing involves blending all the elements of your podcast together, including the music, sound effects, and voiceover. Mastering is the process of enhancing the overall sound quality, making sure the volume is consistent throughout, and preparing the final file for distribution.

### *Adding ID3 tags*

ID3 tags are metadata that provide information about your podcast, such as the title, artist, album, and artwork. These tags are important for organizing and categorizing your podcast, and for SEO purposes.

In conclusion, audio editing is a crucial aspect of podcast production. It's important to take the time to clean up, trim, and polish your audio to make it sound professional and engaging to your listeners. By using the right software, tools, and techniques, you can create a podcast that stands out and draws in a loyal audience.

# TWENTY-NINE

# Podcasting is Like Your Own Website

Podcasting is often compared to social media or YouTube, but in reality, it is more like having your own website. While social media and YouTube provide a platform for hosting content, they ultimately own and control the content you create. In contrast, with podcasting, you have control over your content and how it is distributed.

## *The Importance of Self-Hosting*

One of the biggest advantages of podcasting is that you can self-host your content. Unlike social media or YouTube, where your content is hosted on someone else's platform when you self-host your podcast, you have complete control over your content. This means that you can decide how your content is distributed, who can access it, and what kind of advertisements or monetization methods you want to use.

### *The Benefits of Owning Your Platform*

Another advantage of self-hosting your podcast is that you have complete ownership of your platform. You don't have to worry about a platform banning your account or taking down your content because of a policy violation. This also means that you don't have to worry about changes to the algorithm or platform policies that could impact your audience reach or revenue potential.

### *Choosing the Right Hosting Platform*

When it comes to self-hosting your podcast, you have a variety of options available. Some popular podcast hosting platforms include Libsyn, Buzzsprout, and Blubrry. These platforms provide a variety of features, including analytics, distribution to major podcast directories, and support for monetization.

### *Building Your Own Website*

In addition to self-hosting your podcast, you may also choose to build your own website to complement your podcast. This can provide a centralized location for your content and allow you to build a community around your podcast. You can use your website to share additional content, sell merchandise, or offer premium content to subscribers.

Overall, podcasting provides a unique opportunity to build your own platform and have complete control over your content. By self-hosting your podcast and building your own website, you can create a long-lasting presence online and reach a dedicated audience of listeners who are passionate about your content.

# THIRTY

# Podcast Websites

In today's digital age, having a website for your podcast can be an essential element for success. In this chapter, we'll explore the importance of a podcast website and the various options available to create one.

## *The Importance of a Podcast Website*

- Establishes a professional presence for your podcast
- Provides a central hub for your listeners to access your episodes, show notes, and other content
- Helps with search engine optimization (SEO) to increase your discoverability
- Allows for additional opportunities to monetize your podcast, such as sponsorships, merchandise, and donations
- Provides analytics to track your audience and engagement

## *Creating a Podcast Website There are several options available to create a website for your podcast:*

**A. Self-Hosted WordPress Site**

Provides complete control and flexibility over your website's design and functionality

Requires a domain name and hosting plan, which can be obtained through various providers

WordPress has various podcast-specific plugins available to simplify the process of adding episodes and other podcast-related content

**B. Podcast Hosting Platform Website**

Many podcast hosting platforms, such as Buzzsprout, Libsyn, and Podbean, offer website options as part of their service

These options typically provide a streamlined way to display your episodes and show notes, but may have limited customization options

**C. Website Builders**

Website builders, such as Wix, Squarespace, and Weebly, offer easy-to-use tools to create a website without the need for coding knowledge

Some website builders also offer podcast-specific templates and integrations

## *Elements of a Great Podcast Website*

- Clear and visually appealing design
- Easy navigation and access to episodes and show notes
- Links to subscribe to your podcast on various platforms

- Information about the host(s) and guests
- Contact information for the host(s) and inquiries
- Calls-to-action for listener engagement and monetization opportunities
- Analytics and tracking tools

## *Conclusion*

Creating a website for your podcast can be a crucial element for success in today's digital landscape. It provides a professional presence for your podcast, helps with discoverability and monetization, and provides a central hub for your listeners to access your content. With various options available, there is no excuse not to have a website for your podcast.

# THIRTY-ONE

# Transcribing Podcast Episodes

Transcription refers to the process of converting spoken words into written text. In podcasting, transcription involves creating a written record of your podcast episodes. While transcribing your episodes may seem like a daunting task, it can offer several benefits to your podcast.

In this chapter, we will discuss the importance of transcribing your podcast episodes and the different methods and tools available for transcribing.

### *Why transcribe your podcast episodes?*

- Accessibility: Transcribing your podcast episodes makes them accessible to people who are deaf or hard of hearing. This helps to make your content inclusive and reach a wider audience.

- SEO: Transcripts can also help with search engine optimization (SEO) by providing search engines with more text to index. This can make it easier for people to find your podcast through search engines.
- Repurposing content: Transcriptions can also be repurposed as blog posts, articles, or even e-books. This can help to increase your content output and provide additional value to your audience.

### *Manual Transcription*

Manual transcription involves listening to your podcast episode and typing out the words spoken. This can be time-consuming and requires a lot of effort.

However, it can be beneficial if you want to have complete control over the transcription and ensure accuracy.

### *Automatic Transcription*

Automatic transcription involves using software or tools to transcribe your podcast episodes. These tools use speech recognition technology to convert spoken words into text.

While automatic transcription can save time, it may not always be accurate, especially with accents or background noise.

Some examples of automatic transcription tools include Descript, Otter.ai, and Sonix.

### *Hiring a Transcriptionist*

If you don't want to transcribe your podcast episodes yourself or use automatic transcription tools, you can hire a transcriptionist.

Hiring a transcriptionist can ensure accuracy and save you time. However, it can also be more expensive compared to manual or automatic transcription.

## *Tips for Transcribing Your Podcast Episodes*

- Use timestamps: Using timestamps can help you keep track of where you are in the episode and make it easier to edit.
- Choose the right tool: Choose a transcription tool or service that best suits your needs and budget.
- Proofread and edit: Transcriptions may contain errors, so it's important to proofread and edit them for accuracy.

In conclusion, transcribing your podcast episodes can provide several benefits and help you reach a wider audience. Whether you choose to manually transcribe your episodes, use automatic transcription tools, or hire a transcriptionist, make sure to choose a method that works best for you and your podcast.

# THIRTY-TWO
# Podcast Show Notes

When it comes to podcasting, show notes play an important role in increasing the visibility of your podcast. Show notes are basically a summary of your podcast episode along with some additional information such as links to resources, quotes from the guest, timestamps, etc. In this chapter, we will discuss the importance of show notes and how to write them effectively.

## *Why Show Notes are Important?*

Show notes help your listeners to quickly understand what your podcast is about and decide whether they want to listen to it or not. They also help in improving your search engine optimization (SEO) as search engines can crawl through the show notes and understand what your episode is all about. Additionally, show notes provide a way for your listeners to engage with your content even after they have finished listening to the episode.

### *What to Include in Show Notes?*

Your show notes should include a brief summary of the episode along with some additional information that will make it easier for your listeners to engage with your content. Some of the things that you can include in your show notes are:

- Brief summary of the episode
- Timestamps for important parts of the episode
- Links to resources mentioned in the episode
- Quotes from the guest
- Additional information that was not discussed in the episode but is relevant to the topic
- Social media handles and website links of the guest
- Calls to action (CTAs) for your listeners to engage with your content further.

### *How to Write Effective Show Notes?*

Writing effective show notes can take some time and effort but it is worth it as it can help you in promoting your podcast effectively. Here are some tips for writing effective show notes:

- Start with a brief summary of the episode that highlights the main points covered in the episode.
- Use bullet points to break down the content of the episode into smaller chunks for better readability.
- Use headings and subheadings to organize the content and make it easier to skim through.

- Include timestamps for important parts of the episode so that listeners can easily find what they are looking for.
- Use quotes from the guest to highlight important points and make the show notes more engaging.
- Include links to resources mentioned in the episode so that listeners can easily access them.
- Use a conversational tone while writing the show notes to make them more relatable and engaging.
- End with a call to action (CTA) that encourages your listeners to engage with your content further.

## *Tools to Help You Write Show Notes?*

There are several tools available online that can help you in writing effective show notes. Here are some of the popular ones:

- Google Docs: Google Docs is a free online word processor that you can use to write and share your show notes with your team members.
- Evernote: Evernote is a note-taking app that you can use to organize your show notes and collaborate with your team members.
- Notion: Notion is an all-in-one workspace that you can use to write and organize your show notes, create to-do lists, and collaborate with your team members.
- Trello: Trello is a project management tool that you can use to organize your show notes and collaborate with your team members.

In conclusion, show notes are an important part of promoting your podcast and engaging with your listeners. By following the tips mentioned in this chapter and using the right tools, you can create effective show notes that will help you in growing your podcast audience.

# THIRTY-THREE

# VIDEO PODCASTS

In recent years, video podcasts have gained popularity alongside audio-only podcasts. Video podcasts provide an opportunity to engage with your audience visually and can attract a different audience from audio-only podcasts. In this chapter, we will discuss the benefits of video podcasts and how to create a successful video podcast.

## *What are Video Podcasts?*

Video podcasts, also known as vodcasts, are a form of podcast that incorporates video. Unlike audio-only podcasts, video podcasts allow creators to engage with their audience visually. Video podcasts are often recorded in a studio or on location and can include interviews, demonstrations, and other visual content.

## *Benefits of Video Podcasts*

Video podcasts offer several benefits over audio-only podcasts. Some of the benefits include:

- Greater audience engagement: Video podcasts allow creators to connect with their audience visually, creating a more engaging experience.
- Increased reach: Video podcasts can be shared on multiple platforms, including YouTube and social media, increasing the potential reach of your content.
- Monetization opportunities: Video podcasts can be monetized through sponsorships, advertising, and other revenue streams.
- Improved discoverability: Video podcasts have better SEO potential as they include visual content, metadata, and closed captioning.

## *Tips for Creating a Successful Video Podcast*

Creating a successful video podcast requires more planning and preparation than an audio-only podcast. Some tips for creating a successful video podcast include:

- Choosing the right equipment: Video podcasts require cameras, lighting, and other equipment to produce high-quality content.
- Planning visual content: Video podcasts require visual content, such as graphics, animations, and b-roll footage. It's important to plan out the visual elements ahead of time.
- Editing for visual impact: Video podcasts require editing to create a polished final product. In addition to audio editing, video podcasts require visual editing to create a compelling viewing experience.
- Optimizing for different platforms: Video podcasts can be shared on multiple platforms, but each platform has

different requirements for video size, aspect ratio, and file type. It's important to optimize your video podcast for each platform.

- Incorporating closed captioning: Closed captioning is important for accessibility and SEO. It's important to include closed captioning in your video podcast.

## *Conclusion*

Video podcasts offer an opportunity to engage with your audience visually and attract a different audience from audio-only podcasts. To create a successful video podcast, it's important to choose the right equipment, plan visual content, edit for visual impact, optimize for different platforms, and incorporate closed captioning. With the right approach, video podcasts can be a valuable addition to your podcasting strategy.

# THIRTY-FOUR

# How to Get Podcast Guests?

Podcasts can be a great platform to share your knowledge, expertise, and stories with your listeners. However, to keep your content engaging and fresh, it's essential to invite guests to your podcast. Guests not only add credibility to your show but also bring new perspectives and ideas that your audience can benefit from. In this chapter, we will discuss how you can get guests for your podcast.

### *Define Your Guest Profile*

Before you start reaching out to potential guests, it's essential to define the profile of the guests you want to have on your podcast. You need to consider the topics that you cover in your podcast and identify the experts, authors, influencers, or industry leaders that can provide valuable insights on those topics.

### *Leverage Your Network*

Your personal and professional network can be an excellent source of potential guests. Reach out to your friends, colleagues, or acquaintances who have knowledge or expertise in your niche. You can also join online communities or forums related to your industry to connect with potential guests.

### *Cold Outreach*

If you don't have any direct connections to potential guests, cold outreach can be an effective way to get guests for your podcast. You can find potential guests on LinkedIn, Twitter, or other social media platforms, and send them a personalized message about your podcast and why you think they would be a great fit.

### *Use Podcast Guest Services*

There are many podcast guest services available that can help you connect with potential guests. These services allow you to search for guests based on topics, expertise, and availability. Some popular podcast guest services include MatchMaker.fm, PodMatch, and PodcastGuests.com.

### *Attend Conferences or Events*

Attending industry conferences or events can be a great way to meet potential guests in person. You can network with speakers or attendees and invite them to be guests on your podcast.

## *Offer Value*

When reaching out to potential guests, it's essential to offer them value. Explain how being a guest on your podcast can help them reach a new audience or position themselves as an authority in their niche. You can also offer to promote their work or provide them with a copy of the episode for their own use.

## *Follow Up*

Following up is crucial when it comes to securing guests for your podcast. If you don't receive a response to your initial outreach, follow up with a polite reminder. Persistence and consistency can help you get the guests you want for your podcast.

In conclusion, inviting guests to your podcast can add value to your content and help you grow your audience. By defining your guest profile, leveraging your network, using podcast guest services, attending events, offering value, and following up, you can get the guests you want for your podcast.

# THIRTY-FIVE

# WHAT QUESTIONS TO ASK YOUR GUEST?

Asking the right questions to your podcast guests can make all the difference in creating an engaging and informative episode. Here are some subsections to consider when coming up with questions:

### *Introduction and Background:*

- Can you tell us a bit about yourself and your background?
- How did you get into your current profession or industry?
- What inspired you to pursue this career?

## *Expertise and Opinion:*

- What are your thoughts on [topic related to guest's expertise]?
- Can you share any tips or advice for [related topic]?
- What do you think is the future of [related industry]?

## *Personal Experiences:*

- Can you share a personal experience that taught you a valuable lesson?
- What has been your biggest challenge in your career and how did you overcome it?
- Can you share a success story or accomplishment that you are proud of?

## *Current Events:*

- What are your thoughts on the recent [news event related to guest's industry or expertise]?
- How has your industry been impacted by [current event]?
- What do you think is the most important issue facing your industry right now?

## *Fun and Personal:*

- What do you like to do in your free time?
- Can you share a fun or interesting fact about yourself that most people don't know?
- What is your favorite book, movie, or TV show and why?

By incorporating these types of questions into your podcast interviews, you can create a well-rounded and engaging episode that your listeners will enjoy. Remember to tailor your questions to your guest's expertise and interests to keep the conversation flowing naturally.

# THIRTY-SIX

# Tools & Softwares for Remote Podcast Guest Interviews

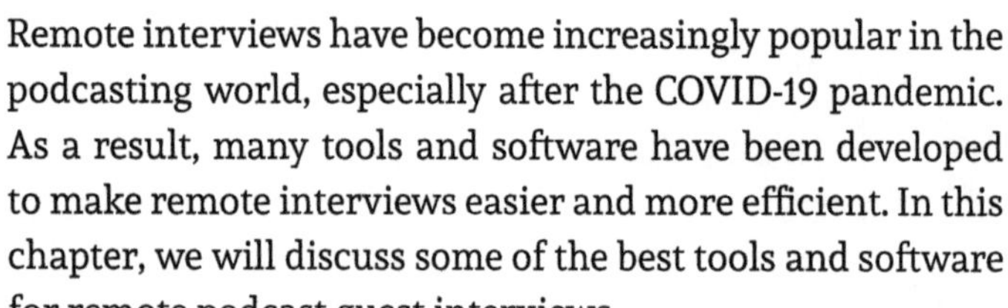

Remote interviews have become increasingly popular in the podcasting world, especially after the COVID-19 pandemic. As a result, many tools and software have been developed to make remote interviews easier and more efficient. In this chapter, we will discuss some of the best tools and software for remote podcast guest interviews.

### *Skype*

Skype is one of the oldest and most widely used communication tools for remote interviews. It is a free tool that allows you to make audio and video calls, share screens, and send files. It is available for Windows, Mac, Android, and iOS devices. Skype has a clear and reliable audio and video quality, making it a great choice for remote interviews.

### *Zoom*

Zoom is a popular video conferencing tool that is commonly used for remote interviews. It allows you to make video and audio calls, share screens, and record your interviews. Zoom also provides features like breakout rooms and virtual backgrounds, making it a great tool for conducting group interviews or adding visual elements to your podcast.

### *Zencastr*

Zencastr is a web-based tool that offers high-quality audio recording for remote interviews. It allows you to record each guest's audio locally, which means you get the best possible quality without any internet disruptions. Zencastr also automatically saves each guest's audio as a separate track, making it easier to edit your podcast.

### *Squadcast*

Squadcast is another web-based tool that offers high-quality audio and video recording for remote interviews. It offers features like live video previews, automatic post-production, and real-time collaboration, making it a great choice for podcasters who want to create a more professional-looking podcast.

## *Riverside.fm*

Riverside.fm is a web-based tool that offers high-quality audio and video recording for remote interviews. It offers features like automatic back-up recordings, studio-quality sound, and video recording in up to 4k resolution, making it a great choice for podcasters who want the highest possible quality for their podcasts.

## *Cleanfeed*

Cleanfeed is a web-based tool that offers high-quality audio recording for remote interviews. It is designed specifically for recording high-quality audio, making it a great choice for podcasters who prioritize audio quality over video. Cleanfeed also allows you to connect multiple guests to the same recording session, making it easier to conduct group interviews.

## *Ringr*

Ringr is a mobile app that allows you to make high-quality audio and video calls with your guests. It is available for both iOS and Android devices and offers features like automatic noise reduction and automatic leveling of audio levels, making it a great choice for podcasters who want to record interviews on the go.

## *Conclusion*

Remote interviews are an essential part of podcasting, and with the right tools and software, you can make them easier and more efficient. Skype, Zoom, Zencastr, Squadcast, Riverside.fm, Cleanfeed, Ringr, and ID3 tagging software are just a few of the many tools and software options available to help you conduct high-quality remote podcast guest interviews. Choose the tools that work best for your podcasting needs and create professional-sounding interviews for your audience.

# THIRTY-SEVEN

# How to Make Money Podcasting?

Podcasting has become an increasingly popular medium for content creators to reach a wide audience and build a loyal following. While many people start podcasting for the love of it, it's also possible to monetize your podcast and turn it into a source of income. In this chapter, we'll explore some of the ways you can make money from podcasting.

### *Sponsorships*

One of the most popular ways to monetize your podcast is through sponsorships. Many businesses and brands are interested in partnering with podcasters to reach their target audience. Sponsorship deals can take various forms, from pre-roll or mid-roll ads to product placements or sponsored segments. To attract sponsors, you'll need to have a significant following and a specific niche audience that aligns with the sponsor's brand.

## *Affiliate Marketing*

Another way to make money from your podcast is through affiliate marketing. This involves promoting other people's products or services and earning a commission on any sales made through your unique affiliate link. Affiliate marketing can be a great way to monetize your podcast without interrupting the listener's experience with ads. Some popular affiliate programs include Amazon Associates and Clickbank.

## *Selling Digital Products*

If you have a loyal following, you can consider creating and selling digital products related to your podcast's topic. This could include e-books, online courses, or memberships. Digital products can be an excellent way to monetize your podcast because you can create them once and sell them repeatedly.

## *Crowdfunding*

Crowdfunding is another option to monetize your podcast. Platforms like Patreon and Kickstarter allow your listeners to support your podcast by making a one-time or recurring donation. In return, you can offer exclusive content or rewards to your supporters.

## *Live Events*

If you have a dedicated following, you can consider hosting live events related to your podcast's topic. This could include meet-and-greets, live recordings, or even conferences. Live events can be an excellent way to monetize your podcast while also engaging with your audience in person.

### *Selling Merchandise*

Selling merchandise related to your podcast can also be a lucrative way to monetize your show. This could include t-shirts, mugs, stickers, or any other merchandise related to your podcast's topic or brand. Sites like Teespring and Spreadshirt make it easy to create and sell merchandise without any upfront costs.

In conclusion, there are many ways to make money from podcasting. Whether you choose sponsorships, affiliate marketing, digital products, crowdfunding, live events, or merchandise sales, the key is to have a loyal following and a unique niche that appeals to your audience.

# THIRTY-EIGHT

# HOW TO GET PODCAST SPONSORS?

If you are looking to monetize your podcast, getting sponsors is a great way to do it. However, getting sponsors for your podcast is not always an easy task. In this chapter, we will discuss some tips on how to get podcast sponsors.

### *Define your audience and niche:*

Before approaching potential sponsors, it is important to define your target audience and niche. This will help you find sponsors that are a good fit for your podcast and will increase your chances of getting a positive response. Consider factors such as age, gender, location, interests, and behaviour to create a clear picture of your ideal listener.

### *Create a media kit:*

A media kit is a document that provides potential sponsors with information about your podcast, including audience demographics, download numbers, and episode topics. A well-designed media kit can help you stand out and increase your chances of getting a sponsor. Make sure to include your contact information so that sponsors can easily get in touch with you.

### *Find potential sponsors:*

Research potential sponsors that align with your niche and target audience. Look for companies that are already advertising on other podcasts or in related industries. You can also use podcast advertising networks such as AdvertiseCast or Podcorn to find potential sponsors.

### *Craft a pitch:*

Once you have identified potential sponsors, craft a pitch that clearly outlines the benefits of sponsoring your podcast. Include information about your audience, the value that your podcast provides, and the reach that you have. Make sure to tailor your pitch to each sponsor and highlight the unique benefits that they will receive by sponsoring your podcast.

### *Negotiate sponsorship terms:*

Once you have secured a sponsor, negotiate the terms of the sponsorship. This can include the length of the sponsorship, the number of ads per episode, and the price. Make sure that the terms are clearly defined in a written agreement to avoid any misunderstandings.

### *Deliver on your promises:*

Make sure to deliver on the promises that you made to your sponsor. This includes mentioning their brand or product in each episode and providing any metrics that were agreed upon. This will help build a positive relationship with your sponsor and increase the chances of future partnerships.

In conclusion, getting podcast sponsors takes time and effort. However, by following the steps outlined above, you can increase your chances of securing a sponsor and monetizing your podcast. Remember to always provide value to your listeners and sponsors, and to be authentic in your approach to sponsorships.

# THIRTY-NINE

# MAKE *MORE* PODCAST MONEY

Promoting affiliate products, sponsors, or your own products in your podcast can be a great way to monetize your show and earn revenue. However, it's important to strike a balance between promoting products and maintaining the quality and integrity of your podcast.

### *Choose Relevant Products or Services*

To promote products or services effectively, they should be relevant to your podcast niche and audience.

Make sure to do your research and choose products or services that align with your values and won't alienate your listeners.

If promoting affiliate products, make sure to disclose your relationship with the company to your audience.

### *Incorporate Product Promotion Strategically*

Don't overload your episodes with product promotions. Make sure to spread them out and incorporate them strategically.

Consider using ad spots, sponsored segments, or product reviews to incorporate product promotion.

Use a call to action (CTA) at the end of each promotion to encourage listeners to check out the product or service.

### *Use Promo Codes or Affiliate Links*

When promoting affiliate products or services, use unique promo codes or affiliate links to track the success of your promotions.

Make sure to disclose any affiliate relationships to your audience and only promote products or services that you genuinely believe in.

Consider negotiating a higher commission rate with your affiliate partners based on the success of your promotions.

### *Leverage Social Media and Email Marketing*

Use your podcast's social media accounts and email list to promote affiliate products or services and drive traffic to your unique promo codes or affiliate links.

Consider creating social media posts or emails specifically for promoting products, and don't forget to include a call to action.

### *Promote Your Own Products or Services*

If you have your own products or services, your podcast can be a great platform to promote them.

Make sure to incorporate promotion strategically and don't overload your episodes with self-promotion.

Use your podcast's social media accounts and email list to promote your products or services and drive traffic to your website.

## *Conclusion*

Promoting affiliate products, sponsors, or your own products can be a great way to monetize your podcast and earn revenue.

However, it's important to choose relevant products or services, incorporate promotions strategically, use promo codes or affiliate links, and leverage social media and email marketing to drive traffic and sales.

# FORTY

# Podcast Networks and How They Help

In the world of podcasting, there are many independent podcasters who create and produce their own content. While this is a great way to get started, it can be challenging to build an audience and find sponsorships on your own. This is where podcast networks come in. In this chapter, we will explore what podcast networks are and how they can help you grow your podcast.

## *What are Podcast Networks?*

Podcast networks are companies or organizations that work with multiple podcasts to provide support, resources, and opportunities for growth. These networks can be large or small, and they may focus on a specific genre or niche. Some networks also offer services such as production, editing, and distribution.

## *How do Podcast Networks help?*

Podcast networks can offer a variety of benefits for podcasters, including:

- Increased Exposure: When you join a podcast network, you have the opportunity to be featured on the network's website, social media, and other marketing channels. This can help you reach a larger audience and gain new listeners.
- Collaborative Opportunities: Podcast networks can facilitate collaborations between podcasts, allowing you to cross-promote each other's shows, share guests, and even produce joint episodes.
- Sponsorship Opportunities: Networks may have established relationships with sponsors, making it easier for you to secure sponsorships for your show.
- Production and Technical Support: Depending on the network, you may have access to resources such as professional editing, sound engineering, and other technical support services.
- Community Support: Being part of a podcast network can provide a sense of community and support, allowing you to connect with other podcasters who are going through similar challenges and experiences.

## *Joining a Podcast Network*

If you are interested in joining a podcast network, here are some things to consider:

- Find a network that aligns with your values and niche: Look for a network that has a similar focus to your podcast and shares your values.
- Research the network's track record: Look for networks that have a history of success and a proven track record of helping their podcasters grow.
- Understand the terms and expectations: Make sure you understand the terms of the agreement and what the network expects from you in terms of content, promotion, and participation.
- Network's Distribution Model: Check how the network distributes the podcast, does it limit the distribution to its network or distribute it widely?

## *Conclusion*

Joining a podcast network can be a great way to grow your podcast and connect with other podcasters. However, it's important to do your research and choose a network that aligns with your values and goals. Remember, the goal of podcasting is to create great content that resonates with your audience, and being part of a network can help you achieve that.

And if you are a podcaster who shares the values and principles that we at Podnity believe in, we are always open to hearing from you and exploring potential collaborations.

# FORTY-ONE

# WHY MOST PODCASTERS NEVER MAKE MONEY?

Podcasting has become an increasingly popular medium for people to express their opinions, share knowledge, and connect with like-minded individuals. However, despite the growing popularity of podcasting, many podcasters struggle to monetize their content and make a sustainable income from their efforts. In this chapter, we will explore some of the reasons why most podcasters never make money.

### *Lack of Consistency*

One of the most significant reasons why many podcasters struggle to make money is due to a lack of consistency in their content creation. Podcasting requires a significant investment of time, effort, and resources. Many podcasters start out with a lot of enthusiasm but quickly lose steam when they realize how much work is involved in creating high-quality content on a regular basis. Without consistency, it is challenging to build a loyal audience and attract sponsors who are willing to invest in your podcast.

### *Lack of Niche Focus*

Another common mistake that podcasters make is failing to focus on a specific niche. The most successful podcasts are those that cater to a particular audience and offer content that is both informative and entertaining. If you are trying to appeal to everyone, you will likely end up appealing to no one. Sponsors are looking for podcasts with a specific target audience, and if you can't provide that, they are unlikely to invest in your podcast.

### *Poor Audio Quality*

The audio quality of your podcast is one of the most important aspects of your content. If your audio is poor, people are unlikely to stick around long enough to listen to your message. You don't need to have the most expensive equipment to achieve good audio quality, but you do need to put effort into creating high-quality audio. If you don't invest in quality audio equipment or editing software, it will show in the final product, and you will struggle to attract sponsors who want to work with professional podcasts.

### *Lack of Marketing*

Even if you create high-quality content consistently and have a focused niche, if you don't market your podcast, no one will know about it. Many podcasters make the mistake of assuming that if they create good content, listeners will naturally find them. But the reality is that there are thousands of other podcasts out there competing for listeners' attention. Without proper marketing, it will be challenging to attract new listeners and sponsors.

## *No Mentorship or System*

Many podcasters never make money because they are trying to figure things out on their own. While it is possible to learn everything you need to know about podcasting through trial and error, it is a time-consuming process. Without a mentor or system to guide you, it is easy to make mistakes and waste time. By joining a community of podcasters or investing in a mentorship program like Podnity, you can learn from the experiences of others who have already been successful in the podcasting industry.

## *Conclusion*

Podcasting can be an incredibly rewarding experience both personally and financially. However, as we have discussed in this chapter, there are many common mistakes that podcasters make that prevent them from monetizing their content successfully. By addressing these issues and investing in yourself through mentorship and community, you can increase your chances of success and achieve your podcasting goals. So, if you want to make money from your podcast and avoid the pitfalls that most podcasters fall into, consider investing in your podcasting education and joining a community of like-minded individuals who can help you achieve your goals.

# What's Next?

Podcasting in India is just getting started.

If you haven't watched my new updated free video training, head over to Podnity.com

Check out our Official Podcast "P for Podcasting" on Streaming Platforms for more valuable content.

*Don't forget to Send me a **Video of You with the Book** at hello@podnity.com and I'll send you back a **Secret Offer** in Return.*

Until we meet again, Happy Podcasting :)

Printed by Libri Plureos GmbH in Hamburg,
Germany